Letter to the Principal:
We Would Really Like...

by Mrs. Wilson's class
with Tony Stead

capstone®
classroom

Have you ever really wanted something for your class or school? In this book, you will read letters that kids have written to their principal asking for different things. You might find some of these letters useful when writing your own letters, asking for something that you want for the school or for your classroom.

April 12

Dear Principal Cohen,

    We need more recess! We need opportunities to play with our friends. Also, it's a good idea if we take a brain break from working so hard. When students have more time at recess, they talk less in class. What else could we do to try to coax you into letting us have more recess?

Sincerely,

Ainsley and Josie

If you let your students stay aut later at recess they will talk less in Class
Brain Breaks are awesome!
we love playing outside so give us more time

April 12

Dear Principal Cohen,

We want to have a class pet. Here are some reasons why we want this.

Our first reason is that children can have company when they are lonely, and if children don't have any friends, they can play with the pet. Don't be concerned, children will not tamper with it.

Our second reason is that kids can read to it and get more fluent in reading if they are having trouble.

Our last reason is that if you have a pet at home, you can teach the class how to be an extraordinary and responsible pet caretaker.

That is why we want a class pet.

Regards,

Madalynn and Sahana

April 13

Dear Principal Cohen,

We would really like to have iPads for every student. We can use them to research, take notes, and take tests. They don't take up much space, and they save time because they will be on our desks.

Yours truly,

Anastasia and David

April 13

Dear Principal Cohen,

    We would like a butterfly garden for our school. We'll help make the garden. If we had a butterfly garden, kids could do butterfly research. There would be a stupendous improvement in grades! Kids would also get to explore the marvelous lives of butterflies. We think butterflies would help kids in science get good grades and learn stuff about butterflies.

Sincerely,

Arden and Cammy

April 13

Dear Principal Cohen,

We would like laptops for each student. If we have them for everyone, the laptops would make testing easier. You don't have to go to the computer lab and worry about schedules. Please consider laptops for our school.

Yours truly,

Eden and Nisha

April 13

Dear Principal Cohen,

    We really want a science lab for our school. We would like to have it because it would have an enormous amount of space for all of our supplies. We would be able to do more experiments. And kids would probably get marvelous grades. Would you please give us a chance to have one? We would really like to have one.

Your students,

Gloria and Kira

We hope that these letters help you get what you want for your classroom or for your school. Remember to always:

- Start your letter with "Dear,"
- Sign your letter with your name, and
- Ask really nicely and give good reasons for what you want.

Good Luck!